WHITEHEAD AND THE MODERN WORLD

Whitehead and the Modern World

Science, Metaphysics, and Civilization

Three Essays on the Thought of
Alfred North Whitehead

by

VICTOR LOWE
CHARLES HARTSHORNE
A. H. JOHNSON

Preface by

A. CORNELIUS BENJAMIN

Boston   •   THE BEACON PRESS   •   *1950*

Copyright, 1950
THE BEACON PRESS

Printed in U.S.A.

Contents

Preface

ALFRED NORTH WHITEHEAD was born at Ramsgate, England, on February 15, 1861. Educated at Trinity College, Cambridge, where he was subsequently appointed lecturer, he later became lecturer in applied mathematics and mechanics at University College, London, and professor of applied mathematics at the Imperial College of Science and Technology. In 1924 he was appointed professor of philosophy at Harvard University, a position which he held until his retirement in 1937. He was the author of many books and articles in the fields of mathematics, logic, and metaphysics. Already the recipient of many honorary degrees from English and American universities, he was awarded in 1945 the British Order of Merit, one of the highest honors which England bestows upon her subjects.

It has been the task of the contributors to this volume to estimate the significance of Whitehead's role in English and American philosophy. Few contemporary thinkers, I am sure, would subscribe to the extravagant claim, sometimes seriously made, that he is the greatest philosopher of all time. Yet no one, I am equally certain, would deny that he made a deep impression on contemporary philosophy. Whereas many authorities would not be willing to admit that Whitehead always expressed his ideas with both clarity and elegance, most of those who have read his writings with sympathetic understanding agree that his views are characterized by a breadth of experience and a depth of insight which are the envy of all aspiring philosophers. It would be absurd to claim that he solved all philosophical problems. Yet when one sees, among the followers of Whitehead, logicians and metaphysicians, scientists and theologians, Bergsonians and intellectualists, one is compelled to admit that he stands almost unique among recent philosophers in the way in which he reconciled opposing strains in modern thought and achieved the unification without eclecticism which is the true philosophical goal.

When philosophers from two continents gathered in New York on December 28, 1947, to participate in the Second Inter-American Congress of Philosophy, they were saddened by the news that Whitehead lay at the brink of death. Even before adjournment three days later, word was received that he had passed quietly away. It therefore seemed fitting to those who were responsible for the planning of the spring program of the Western Division of the American Philosophical Association to devote a special commemorative session to the philosophy of this important thinker. A panel was arranged and three speakers were invited, each to discuss an aspect of Whitehead's work. The symposium took place on May 8, 1948, at Galesburg, Illinois, where the Division met as the guests of Knox College. Because of the interest in the material presented, the excellence of the papers, and the obvious importance of the event, it was voted that an effort be made to publish the addresses, preferably in a single volume. The present book is the result of this action. The papers are here reproduced in substantially the form they had on that occasion.

A. CORNELIUS BENJAMIN
President, Western Division
American Philosophical Association

WHITEHEAD AND THE MODERN WORLD

Whitehead's Philosophy of Science

By VICTOR LOWE

BOTH AS AN INVESTIGATOR of the foundations of mathematics and as a philosopher, Alfred North Whitehead projected great changes in the whole field of logic and scientific method. His contribution is very obviously a subject which cannot be covered in a short essay. I shall pass over those aspects which would more appropriately be presented, with the help of a big blackboard, before the Association for Symbolic Logic, and concentrate on Whitehead's philosophy of science.

Whitehead had a keen sense of the imperfection of his results, their need of criticism and revision. He used to remark that all he had written was merely a set of suggestions. His attitude was, "Take it from here." Yet he could say, speaking of his divergence from the current operationalist way of setting up geometry as a physical science: "I'm sure I'm right" — and Einstein wrong. He could, in short, be quite sure of the soundness of his general approach to a topic. We, his readers, tend to survey Whitehead's results (for which he claimed so little), see which one (or possibly two) can be fitted into our approaches to the problems of philosophy, and dismiss the rest. Our attention to *his* approach begins and ends with the remark that Whitehead was a man of high genius —

3

and, presumably, low utility. We make an end of his work by treating it as an end in itself, not as means withal. Yet to call a man an intellectual genius is to admit that his mode of thought possesses some unusual virtue. It is up to us to regard our ways as not entirely adequate and give his a trial, however hard that may be. If we are not willing to do this, we may as well stop paying tribute to his genius.

When we concentrate on Whitehead's approach to philosophical problems rather than on his results, we find two main characteristics which make it difficult for us to come up to his level. One is his obvious bold rationalism, which he defined as the hope "that we fail to find in experience any elements intrinsically incapable of exhibition as examples of general theory."[1] The other is an unusual kind and degree of concreteness. This second characteristic of his has also been widely felt. For example, Jacques Barzun not long ago wrote of Whitehead in *Harper's Magazine:*

> Even when his prose is full of snarls and knots, which is usually the result of trying to tame original ideas, one always has the sense of his direct contact with experience, of his concreteness.
>
> This last quality is what is so conspicuously lacking in what is offered us today as thought. We like to believe that it is the Whiteheads of this world who are "abstract thinkers" and need to be brought down to earth. The fact is, only a great mind has the secret of being in touch with things; the abstract ones are the run-of-the-mill philosophers . . . , and the breed becomes more abstract as we reach the pseudos . . . ; it is your plain fellow whose

---

[1] *Process and Reality* (Cambridge, England, 1929), Part II, chap. 1, § II, p. 57.

head is a gas balloon, and who can only be brought down to earth by being exploded.[2]

The memorial notice of Whitehead in *Philosophy and Phenomenological Research* contains the remark, "In the philosophy of science, Whitehead's major contribution consists of 'The Principle of Extensive Abstraction.'" One might wish to qualify this statement; but I think that if we consider the *method* of this "extensive abstraction" we shall see how Whitehead's approach to the philosophy of science, quite as well as his metaphysics, shows a unique combination of theory and concreteness. The usual expositions of extensive abstraction treat it simply as an epistemological device (for replacing inferred by constructed entities), and do not fully catch its broader significance.

"Extensive abstraction" is the technical instrument which Whitehead invented for defining, in terms of relationships evident in the perceptual flux, those deceptively simple concepts of space and time, such as "point," "line," and "instant," in terms of which all exact natural science is expressed. Whitehead's work on this problem, or parts of it, ran from 1905 to 1929, and some of this work was once intended for the fourth volume, on geometry, which he was to contribute to *Principia Mathematica*.[3] In the peculiar place it holds in the general history of its problem, the work on extensive abstraction resembles that great book. Inquiry into the relation of geometry to our experience of nature has if anything a longer history than inquiry into the logical foundations of mathematics. Pro-

---

2 First page of "New Books," issue of March, 1948.

3 Cf. Bertrand Russell, *Our Knowledge of the External World*, preface to first ed. (New York and London, 1914).

tagoras, as we know from Aristotle's approving report, cited the fact that a hoop does not touch a rod merely at one point, to show that the geometer's straight lines and circles do not exist in nature; and Heath thinks that one of Democritus' lost works was probably directed against this sort of criticism.[4] Now, just as the authors of *Principia Mathematica* undertook actually to derive mathematical concepts from logical concepts — actually deduce them, no matter how great the labor — so Whitehead with his method of extensive abstraction undertook to execute some actual derivations instead of merely continuing a discussion begun in Socratic times. His was a rationalism that *went to work*.

The general acceptance of relational conceptions of space and time should have brought such work into being before a Whitehead appeared. According to the relational point of view, anyone who makes a statement about a point P in physical space is really talking about a certain set of relations between extended things. What are these relata and relations? By this formulation of the problem,[5] the interest in "bridging the gap" between spatial experience and scientific concepts is centered upon a demand for a definition of the point of physical space, i.e., the space in which natural phenomena occur, the space which the mathematical physicist has in mind when he writes ordinary differential equations, and the engineer when he plots a curve. Similar definitions are demanded for all other

---

[4] Aristotle, *Metaphysics*, B 2 998a2; Sir Thomas Heath, *History of Greek Mathematics* (Oxford, 1921) , I, 179. Those who study Whitehead's theory of extensive abstraction with care will find that the problem of tangent boundaries was the very one which gave him most trouble!

[5] To be found in *The Aims of Education*, pp. 235f; *An Enquiry Concerning the Principles of Natural Knowledge*, Art. 2.1; *Concept of Nature*, p. 136.

"ideal" spatial entities and for the instant of time and
the point of space-time, but so far as this crucial ideality is
concerned, the point may serve as the representative of
them all. This is the only instance of the method which
I can go into here. It is also the one regularly chosen
for discussion by Whitehead's critics.

An adequate exploration and evaluation of Whitehead's
work with extensive abstraction must go back at least to
the papers he wrote in 1915, 1916, and 1917,[6] and forward
through *Process and Reality*. Right now I shall summarize
only the most familiar version — the one contained in
his *Principles of Natural Knowledge*.[7]

Whitehead there began with a relation of "extension"
holding among events. We continually observe that one
event extends over or encloses another, either spatially or
temporally or in both ways. Since we are now ignoring
the temporal dimension, we may substitute the word "volume" for "event," provided we remember that the word
does not stand for the volumes of pure geometry, but for
portions of the expanse of nature displayed to perception,
like this room. Whitehead assumes that the relation of
"extending over" is transitive[8] and asymmetrical; that its
field is "compact" or "dense";[9] that every volume encloses
other volumes and is itself enclosed by other volumes; and

---

6 Published as chaps. 6, 7, and 8 of *The Organization of Thought* (London, 1917), and reprinted with slight omissions as chaps. 8, 9, and 10
of *Aims of Education*.

7 A condensed summary of Whitehead's theory of extensive abstraction
in its more powerful later form as well, and in its general application to
space-time, is now available in chap. 3 of William W. Hammerschmidt's
admirable monograph, *Whitehead's Philosophy of Time* (New York, 1947).

8 I.e., if *A* extends over *B* and *B* extends over *C*, then *A* extends over *C*.

9 I.e., between any two volumes, one of which encloses another, there is
a third which encloses the second and is enclosed by the first.

that for any two volumes there exists a third enclosing
them both.[10]

The next step in the method is the definition of what
Whitehead called an "abstractive set" of volumes. An
example is the set of all spheres concentric to a certain
point. But neither the notion of the point, nor that of
any regular geometrical figure, enters into the definition.
An abstractive set is defined[11] by only two conditions:
First, of any two of its volumes, one encloses the other.
Second, there is no volume which is a common part of
every volume of the set; thus the set has no minimum
volume, but is an infinite series whose members diminish
without end. By ingenious technical devices, Whitehead
gathered abstractive sets into classes and into types of
classes, so that sets diminishing in all three dimensions, and
so defining points, are distinguished from sets diminishing in fewer dimensions and so defining lines and planes.
We are then ready to translate any statement about points

---

10 See *Principles of Natural Knowledge,* Art. 27.1 for Whitehead's exact
formulation. Art. 17.4 shows that he made one more assumption — that
volumes have exact demarcations, instead of the vague boundaries which
they exhibit in perception. This assumption complicated his task and was
explicitly adopted only after hesitation: see *Aims of Education,* pp. 213f.
Critics were quick to claim that the assumption makes Whitehead's whole
procedure circular. The question is a difficult one. Hammerschmidt, *op.
cit.,* p. 46, gives a possible answer. I incline to think that the necessity of
the assumption is merely, as Whitehead claimed in Art. 17.4 of *Principles
of Natural Knowledge,* that of a postulate implicit in all rational thought
and "every advance towards exact observation, namely that there is
something definite to be known": what has been vaguely perceived is a
"potentially definite" object for knowledge. Perhaps circularity is satisfactorily avoided by the procedure used in *Process and Reality* (Part IV,
chap. 2), where Whitehead introduces the idea of regions in exact contact
only as a case to be *excluded* in his definition of a point, which is then
made in terms of non-tangential enclosure and thus does not require the
assertion that any region actually has exact boundaries.

11 *Principles of Natural Knowledge,* Art. 30.1. The set is there called
an "abstractive class."

into a statement about abstractive sets. Whitehead used as an example the statement, "the points A and B are two feet apart."[12] This means that the abstractive sets A and B are such that by going down their tail-ends we can always find a volume x in A and a volume y in B such that the distance between x and y approximates 2 feet within any limit, however small, that we may wish to assign. The abstractive set replaces the notion of a point as an entity radically different from anything known in our experience of the physical world and incompatible with physical existence, but believed to be an ideal limit (a phrase not further analyzed) of diminution of extensions which do contain physical existence.

Whitehead represented his method as "merely the systematization of the instinctive procedure of habitual experience." He wrote:

> The approximate procedure of ordinary life is to seek simplicity of relations among events by the consideration of events sufficiently restricted in extension both as to space and as to time; the events are then "small enough." The procedure of the method of extensive abstraction is to formulate the law by which the approximation is achieved and can be indefinitely continued. The complete series is then defined and we have a "route of approximation."[13]

This approach of Whitehead's to the theory of physical space is plainly analogous to his approach to metaphysics, which he conceived as "nothing but the description of the generalities which apply to all the details of practice."[14]

---

12 *Aims of Education*, p. 216.
13 *Principles of Natural Knowledge*, Art. 18.3.
14 *Process and Reality*, Part I, chap. 1, § V, p. 17.

His general comment on Hume was that instead of sup-
plementing conclusions with an appeal to practice, a
philosopher should put our habitual practice into his
premises. The devilishly hard thing to do, of course, is
to systematize this practice with some completeness. To
Whitehead that meant looking for the types of relata
and relations with which it universally deals, rendering
these into a coherent set of concepts, and deducing implications. Such was his aim in both his philosophy of science
and his metaphysics. John Dewey's *Experience and Nature*
contains a considerable description of our habitual practice, but no such *theory;* and I remember Whitehead's
saying that he didn't see why in heaven's name Dewey
didn't go ahead and construct one.

The proper Deweyan answer to this challenge is fortu-
nately not our business at the moment; it seems fairly
clear that the ideal of science is to systematize our hetero-
genous practice in determining spatial positions into a
universal rule stated in terms of a universally applicable
definition. So I am shocked whenever a critic suggests
that the method of extensive abstraction is quite unnecessary because all that physics ever needs or uses is the
notion of an entity which differs from perfect punctuality
by an extent which is negligible for the purposes of the
occasion. When Professor Ducasse offered this criticism,[15]
he seems to have recognized the desirability of uniting
these many definitions for many occasions into one, for
he went on to offer this general definition: a point is "an
entity the size of which would be undetectable through any

---

15 As one which had occurred to both Professor R. M. Blake and himself:
Report of the *Symposium in Honor of the Seventieth Birthday of Alfred
North Whitehead* (Cambridge: Harvard University Press, 1932), p. 10.

test whatever, and therefore negligible for every purpose."
It is very hard to see how such an entity could be of the
slightest use, or what meaning it gives to such statements
as "The intensity of the electric field at the point P is I."
We do not have to make points entities, but to give a universal definition of this at-a-point-ness, or punctuality,
which stands for an ideal exactness in the determination of
spatial position. The introduction of an eternally undetectable entity is nothing but an interesting example of
reification. I have taken a moment to notice it because it
shows the Nemesis which awaits one kind of anti-White-
headian empiricism — the kind which, lacking Whitehead's
full appreciation of the systematic pursuit of exactness by
science, thinks that no ideally exact concepts are required
in the foundations of physics. Ideal exactness cannot be
shrugged off like that.

But neither can it be assumed. Approximation is the
only way in which we can handle space and time. Many
persons (we may call them, philosophically, intuitionists)
think that Whitehead assumed exact points — otherwise
he would not have been able to construct his abstractive
sets. Certainly no one approximates in a vacuum. The
assumed idea is the idea of "being precisely *there*." That
is what we intend to talk about when we talk about a
point; we imagine the possibility of perfect precision. But
— how possible? This is the idea of an undefined superlative not exemplified in experience. All that we experience
is the comparative, "being in this smaller volume." The
definition and realization of the ideal, the superlative,
can be achieved only by an unending series of compara-
tives. That is the lesson of extensive abstraction; and I
know of no one who has taught this lesson, both in the

philosophy of physical science and in that of other human activities — such as politics — better than Whitehead. The advantage enjoyed by physical science is the double one, that our emotions are not involved, and that the subject matter permits us to "convert [the] process of approximation into an instrument of exact thought."[16]

It must not be supposed that there is a simple, perfect idea of punctuality which sits in judgment on these approximations. No such idea is necessary or statable. In Whitehead's view, our most exact knowledge of basic concepts is a systematic formulation, as exact as may be, of relations universally "had" in direct experience.

I think most scientists would say, offhand, that Whitehead's definition of a point was unnecessary. They would distinguish instead two meanings for "point," one purely abstract, the other concrete. The former is provided by such a set of postulates for geometry as Thorstein Veblen's, published in *Monographs on Modern Mathematics*. "Point" there is the sole undefined relatum; what it means is *any* thing, spatial or non-spatial, which conforms to the postulates. The concrete meaning is obtained by turning to actual space and pointing at such visible extended things as chalk-dots on a blackboard; and the two meanings are united by the observation that experiments with the chalk-dots reveal an approximate exemplification of the point-properties laid down in the formal postulates. Unfortunately the mathematical physicist, for whose sake the two meanings were united, will observe that in the sense in which

---

16 From *Principles of Natural Knowledge*, Art. 18.3, where this object of the method of extensive abstraction is compared to that of the differential calculus. The comparison with politics was a favorite one in Whitehead's lectures at Harvard. The answer to the intuitionist is drawn from my notes of Whitehead's lectures in the spring of 1937.

he uses the word "point" in his equations, the chalk-dot is itself a volume composed of points. What has been left out of the account is that "unconscious act of speculative thought"[17] by which the physicist has conceived the observed dot in this way. It *can* be included and made explicit — by taking the dot as the large end of one of Whitehead's abstractive sets. Obviously the same omission is made if, with the operationists, we take our concrete meaning from a very fine mark on a special rod kept under glass in a laboratory or a government bureau. We are not given a meaning for that punctuality which is potentially present in every bit of space, rod or no rod.

Thus Whitehead's concreteness is, that the spaciness of space is in his geometry from the start. Furthermore, his abstractive sets have the logical properties in virtue of which points form a continuum. The farther reaches of his theory develop the further properties of points and of other geometrical elements, which in Veblen's theory are enunciated in purely abstract terms. There is a union of the formal with an infinitude of specific meanings for the operationist to draw upon.

When John Dewey wrote his *Quest for Certainty,* he thought that "extensive abstraction as a mode of defining things" was "similar in import" to the operationist identification of scientific concepts with sets of operations.[18] He failed to observe that the possibility of the operations of approximation, by which Whitehead defines a point, depends entirely on the properties of the relation of "extending over," which is a directly observed relation. There are also other divergences; an interesting paper could be

---

17 Whitehead's phrase: see *Aims of Education,* pp. 157f., 245f.
18 Page 111 and note.

written on the similarities and contrasts between Whitehead's realistic approach and Dewey's instrumentalist approach to the scientific concepts of space and time. Dewey
sticks close to what the scientist consciously does; Whitehead reminds him of what he unconsciously assumes. When
Dewey regards "space" in physics as a name given to
operations possible with respect to things having the quality of spaciousness, the physicist says, "Yes"; and, thinking
of nothing useful to say about this quality of spaciousness,
turns at once to a yardstick. Whitehead is the one man in a
million who found that something could be said about
the spaciousness that was in front of the physicist's nose
before he ever thought of that yardstick.

The operationists, for their part, generally reject Whitehead's method in some such words as these of Professor
Lenzen. (I quote from his *Nature of Physical Theory*,
published in 1931; to the best of my knowledge, he has not
repudiated his criticism.) "As a matter of fact the method
of extensive abstraction is purely formal and never comes
in contact with physical reality. Inasmuch as the abstractive sets are defined by postulates, they are just as abstract
as the points of an abstract geometry."[19] So whatever is defined by postulates is *ipso facto* abstract! What a bland
assurance that there can be no theory *of* the concrete!
Theory is purely formal, and must be held apart from
the experienced world until a laboratory use for it is speci-
fied by declaring that a particular physical body (fortu-
nately there available) gives *the* meaning of the theory
for physical reality!

The conflict between this dualistic philosophy and
Whitehead's comes to a head over the definition of con-

---

[19] Page 66.

gruence. Here the operationist declares further that the length of the chosen body is unchangeable by any movement, but that it does vary with temperature; and he defines congruence by the coincidence of pairs of marks. Whitehead was convinced that there is a level of concrete meaning which lies below that of operations, and he confidently hit the operationist (whom he regarded as *the* enemy) with the argument that every operation presupposes perceptions; for example, the use of coincidence as a test for congruence depends on direct intuitions of permanence in respect to congruence. Whitehead had several other arguments, into which I cannot go. But "the enemy" might study and try to answer at least the fourth section of the fifth chapter of Part Four of *Process and Reality.*

Whitehead was thoroughly competent in mathematical physics, but his philosophy was the opposite of a technician's. The technician is always tempted to elevate his best techniques for making tests into sole criteria for basic meaning. He gets away with it because this is the day of the technician. It is also the day of the businessman; and the speech of the operationist is very businesslike. I regret that George Santayana never, to the best of my knowledge, applied his suave sarcasm here; or that S. J. Perelman has not written a parody on the directors of the Physical Corporation, deciding the foundations of science.

Whitehead's empiricism contrasts with yet another, which holds that his abstractive sets are mere ideal constructions — not because they have to do with volumes directly perceived instead of with marks on steel rods, but because no one has ever perceived such a "dense" series of volumes, an infinite number of them below the limits of perception, as define an abstractive set; only pseudo-empiricisms, it is said, deal in "actual infinites." The question thus raised is complex; I can indicate here only two possible answers. First, if the properties Whitehead ascribes to extension are in part hypothetical, the hypothesis can be defended as, in Jean Nicod's phrase, "an intelligible and modest hypothesis."[20] Second, there is the answer suggested by the doctrine of *Process and Reality,* that we experience the space-time continuum as a "systematic real *potentiality."* We perceive an actual spaciousness as a potentiality of *heres* and *theres* unlimited in number. That is part of the perceptual meaning of spaciousness. Only an artificially pure empiricism would insist on excluding this accent of potentiality from the concept of experience.

Self-examination would show, I think, that antagonism to Whitehead's philosophy is usually due to one of the many current doctrines which claim that this or that aspect of experience cannot be conceptualized. The Bergsonian holds that mechanical movement can be analyzed, but not growth. The instrumentalist confines thought to the conditions of present and future experience, and excludes experience in its felt immediacy, which is supremely important but ineffable. Epistemologists of all sorts raise complicated questions about the applicability of concepts to "the given." Then along comes Whitehead with a *theory* of feelings, and a complex unorthodox epistemology (which I have not gone into) , and a cosmology of growth-quanta as the cells of the universe. Why, the man "effs" the ineffable! We resent his flouting of our pet prohibitions.

As for the method of extensive abstraction in particular,

---

[20] *Foundations of Geometry and Induction* (London, 1930) , p. 47.

it met with too facile praise when it first appeared thirty
years ago; for the past twenty years it has suffered un-
deserved neglect. Russell's empiricism of "particulars"
gained more favor than Whitehead's empiricism of "the
general character of our direct experience."[21] The theory
of extensive abstraction is a piece of mathematical logic,
and the mathematical logicians fear that Whitehead opens
the door to the dogmatic assertion of nonsense as a mere
transcript of basic experience, and the only possible transcript. Such politic considerations have no rightful claim
on science. And while it *would* be dogmatic to say that our
basic experience of space and time can be formulated
in only one way, Whitehead always insisted that there
were a variety of ways. His own definitions of points and
instants in terms of the relation of enclosure among events
were shown by Theodore de Laguna to contradict our
direct experience by entailing a ridiculous degree of dependence of spatial meanings on temporal meanings.[22] In
Process and Reality Whitehead avoided this by beginning
with a different relation, which he called "extensive connection" among "regions." Later he expressed a private
opinion that the relation of betweenness, holding among
regions, would be still better.

I hope that someone skilled in mathematical logic will
soon use that suggestion, rewrite the whole of the deductive

---

21 This phrase, expressive of the empiricism of all Whitehead's philosophical writings, is drawn from *The Principle of Relativity*, p. 4. Con-
sonance with this general character is there insisted upon as one of "the
two gauges through which every [scientific] theory must pass"; the other,
"the habitual working gauge of science," is of course the successful prediction of a variety of specific phenomena.

22 *Philosophical Review*, XXX (1921), 217. Of course this defect of
the theory could not appear in our exposition, because (unlike Whitehead) we artificially eliminated the temporal dimension from the start.

theory of space-time contained in Part Four of *Process*
(which Whitehead left in a very inelegant and sometimes
confused form), and publish it separately. The theory
culminates in a definition of a straight line, made without
reference to measurement. According to a letter which
Professor F. S. C. Northrop recently received from George
Temple, Professor of Mathematics in the University of
London (and a former pupil of Whitehead), mathema-
ticians have up to now done nothing with Whitehead's
definition. In view of the existing departmentalization
of disciplines, nothing so important to mathematical
science as this should be allowed to remain badly stated
on page 465[23] of a book on metaphysics.

I have spoken of the similarity between Whitehead's
approach to the philosophy of science and his approach to
metaphysics. But there is more than a similarity. As he
developed his philosophy of science, he placed it in a
metaphysical setting, so much so that in his later years he
sometimes said that he didn't really think there was such
a subject as the philosophy of science. My choice of the
method of extensive abstraction for illustrative purposes
may have given a misleading impression of Whitehead; for
in the derivation of the concept of a point from the general character of our conscious perceptions of space, metaphysical considerations are irrelevant — the abstraction
of space from process has already been made. Whatever
may be the full story of the occurrence of these perceptions,
the spatial relatedness which they display is an ultimate
datum for science, as Whitehead always insisted. But after
all the perceptions do *occur* as natural events, and the static
display *is* implicated in the process of nature. When we

---

23 Page 432 in the English edition.

try to understand the relation of the display to the process, we are addressing "the nature of things." There is no escape, and Whitehead sought none. His general philosophy of science cannot be separated from his metaphysics.[24]

To balance the picture, suppose we briefly consider Whitehead's approach to causality and induction. There can no more be a natural science without causal laws in the form of functional correlations than there can be a mathematical physics without equations whose variables are interpretable as space-coordinates. But to express what we *mean* by space, Whitehead held, we must go behind those variables to the general character of space-perception.[25] Neither can causal laws reveal the nature of causality. Causality is a character of every experience or it is no generic character of nature. Whitehead described it as the compulsion of the past on the present. On men's opinions of this, their attitude toward Whitehead's entire philosophy mainly depends. I think that this is the best single thing Whitehead did, but I am not so foolish as to try to change your opinions on the subject. In the spirit of Whitehead himself, let me rather suggest, to those who have not *a priori* dismissed his theory of causality, two respects in which it might profit by criticism. First, the

---

[24] Anyone who discusses Whitehead's philosophy of science (or even of space-time) as if it were entirely contained in the books he published on that subject between 1919 and 1922 is guilty of criminal laziness, and is grossly unfair to a man who was ever pushing beyond the usual boundaries of inquiry. For a survey of Whitehead's intellectual career as a series of expanding investigations, and a discussion of the connection between Whitehead the mathematician, the philosopher of science, and the metaphysician, my essay on "The Development of Whitehead's Philosophy" (Essay I in *The Philosophy of Alfred North Whitehead,* edited by P. A. Schilpp, 1941) may be consulted.

[25] Cf. (one among many possible references) *Principles of Natural Knowledge,* Art. 10.7.

distinction which he drew between causal experience and presentational experience appears sharper than the facts allow. Second, the methodical connection between causal experience, to which Whitehead remanded us, and the causal laws of science should be filled out more at its upper end.

In Whitehead's view, the inductive logic that is involved in the use of causal laws has a metaphysical ground. This does *not* mean that we cannot make and communicate inductive inferences until we have agreed upon our metaphysics.[26] It means, in Whitehead's own words, that "Either there is something about the immediate occasion which affords knowledge of the past and the future, or we are reduced to utter skepticism as to memory and induction."[27] This strikes me as one of the soundest, most down-to-earth remarks ever made on the problem of induction. If we do not assume that earlier events have powers to affect later events (identified by reference to them), our thought merely dances in some ethereal region. Nothing but suspicion need be accorded any theory of causal induction, however elegant and economical, which, if it were true, would be (like the laws of arithmetic on one interpretation of them) just as true in Plato's heaven as in this world of past, present, and future.

The dependence of a scientist's inductions on metaphysics is a reflection, in his conscious awareness of what he is doing, of his general dependence as a natural scientist

---

26 This doctrine of dependence does however imply that so far as we have not developed a common metaphysics of nature, we have no common awareness of what makes our inductions valid, and are successful only because we act better than we know.

27 *Science and the Modern World,* first American ed., p. 62 (p. 64 in most reprints).

on nature. It is merely superficial to take metaphysics out of this relationship and treat it as if it were tomorrow's weather prediction for Illinois — one more hypothesis awaiting inductive verification, hence itself incapable of supporting inductions. Certainly every metaphysical system is a hypothesis; Whitehead insisted on that.[28] But this fact does not prevent the system, as a cosmology or general Concept of Nature (terms which I prefer to "metaphysics") from including a conceptualization of the traits of nature on which induction depends. To recognize its hypothetical character is but to recognize that the cosmology, as a human product, is an imperfect verbalization of those traits. Experience is dumb; only by speculative trial can the philosopher formulate concepts which express with some adequacy the generic traits of nature which he enjoys. The philosopher must always face the questions, "Does this speculative Concept of Nature accord with the persistent character of our experience and practice?" and "Does it work well as a frame of reference for thought in the special sciences?"

I am quite aware that I am defending Whitehead's position with broad generalities. I believe that the position can be analyzed and argued in as meticulous a manner as that which distinguishes C. I. Lewis among living philosophers. This work I strongly recommend. In particular, it should be possible to do full justice to the further dependence of the inductive process on the ways in which the scientist defines the terms of his questions. This element is most obvious in deductive logic, where it accounts for the apparent autonomous subsistence of logical prin-

---

28 Cf. *Process and Reality*, Preface and Part I, chap. 1; *Adventures of Ideas*, pp. 285f., and, more generally, chaps. 9 and 15.

ciples independent of nature. But, to borrow a word from Santayana, it would be a mere egotism to leave nature out of that story too.

When a human being tries to formulate a general Concept of Nature, he is bound to mix his favorite preconceptions into his descriptive generalizations of experience. As I see it, Whitehead's preconceptions were largely Platonic and religious. The weakest part of his theory of induction is his addition, in *Process and Reality*, of an appeal to a theological ground.[29] I personally am convinced that if there is a God who has anything to do with nature, he is the sort of God who appears in Whitehead's system. But the experiment of naturalizing Whitehead's philosophy of nature ought to be tried. That is one of the hardest, biggest, and probably one of the most rewarding tasks our generation can undertake.

It has often been said that the wise scientist is the one who, at the height of his triumph, confesses his abysmal ignorance. The thought were better put positively: a scientist is philosophical if he enjoys a sense of the tremendous variety of unexplored ideas lying beyond those used in current explanations. One of the greatest possible values for science of a system of philosophy is its cultivation of that sense. The scope and the entire temper of Whitehead's philosophy admirably fit it for this service. But also, the general categories of thought which a philosophy conveys may sometimes turn a scientist's imagination in just the direction needed for solving his problems. Though Whitehead's philosophy has been ignored by the vast majority of scientists, there are instances of such applications. I am thinking, for example, of a paper on "The Organiza-

---

[29] Part II, chap. 9, § VIII.

tion of a Story and a Tale," published by a student of
ethnology, the late William Morgan, in Volume LVIII
(1945) of the *Journal of American Folklore;* and of W. E.
Agar's book, *A Contribution to the Theory of the Living
Organism.*[30] Not that these instances might not turn out
to be duds. Certainly they might. Whitehead claimed no
indispensability or "correctness" for his results. He would
have been satisfied were scientists more willing to acknowl-
edge the principles — amply confirmed by the history of
science — that the fruitfulness of observation depends on
having general schemes of thought in mind, and that it
is "treason to the future" to lay down limits in advance
for such schemes. "A self-satisfied rationalism," he wrote,
"is in effect a form of anti-rationalism."[31]

The self-satisfaction reflects an uncritical worship of
clarity and "reliable information." I am depressed by the
way books on scientific method put a halo around "reliable
information." To Whitehead this meant a trivialization
of science, the death of intellectual adventure.[32] Contrary
to a widespread opinion, he never thought clarity was
anything but desirable. What he taught was that scientific
and philosophic theory, like the infinite abstractive sets
by which he defined punctuality, can never achieve perfect
precision and must never abandon its pursuit. (If only
the universe allowed the philosopher to concentrate on
the definition of one character to the exclusion of others,
as in our example we concentrated on punctuality!) In
this pursuit — in all our discussions — " 'clear' always

---

[30] Melbourne, 1943; p. 95 and *passim*.
[31] *Science and the Modern World*, first American ed., p. 281 (p. 289 in most reprints) .
[32] These phrases are probably unconscious quotations from Whitehead.

means 'clear enough' ";[33] even as precision in the determination of spatial position always means "precise enough." This relativity of clarity, springing from the fact that we are (as Whitehead liked to say) finite creatures living in an incompletely analyzed environment, should be the first principle of all philosophic thought. It dominated Whitehead's mind. The result of its interfusion with his concreteness and his adventurous rationalism was a quality of wisdom not elsewhere to be found in the philosophy of science.

---

[33] I have been unable to find the source of this statement of Whitehead's. For the general doctrine, see *Modes of Thought*, Lectures I-VI, and many passages in his other philosophic writings (e.g., *Adventures of Ideas*, p. 185).

Whitehead's Metaphysics

By CHARLES HARTSHORNE

WHAT HAS WHITEHEAD CONTRIBUTED to the subjects of metaphysics and cosmology? By "metaphysics" I mean the study of the necessary, eternal, completely universal aspects of reality; by "cosmology," the attempt, combining metaphysics and scientific knowledge, to discern the large, comparatively universal features of nature as now constituted. Cosmology is science running more risks than usual, or indulging in greater vagueness, in order to achieve a more complete and rounded picture; but the risks and the vagueness may be less if some clarity has been achieved as to what makes metaphysical sense, as opposed to the confusion that results when we attempt to escape the inescapable or necessary — the metaphysical — traits of being and process.

Whitehead was a metaphysician as well as a cosmologist, and in my opinion supremely great in both roles. Indeed, I see no one since Leibniz to compare with him, and no one at all to compare with him in the adequacy of his conclusions. This of course does not mean that I believe there are no defects in his thinking or writing. (Once, when asked why he did not write more clearly, he replied, "Because I do not think more clearly.") Accurate definition of the merits of a philosophy seems indeed logically impossible without indication of how they are limited or bounded by errors — such as human beings can scarcely avoid. Nevertheless, for good or evil, this essay is written almost solely in praise, rather than criticism, of Whitehead. On this occasion, I am trying to outline some reasons that can be given for the above-suggested high estimate of his importance:

1. Whitehead is a rationalist who formulates and even practices a rational method! Rationalism is the search for views that are of necessity true because, owing to their absolute generality, they have no rational alternative. But the only way to be sure of this is, in every case, to explore the possibility of formulating an alternative. The "rationalists" of the past failed to do so. Leibniz assumes as rationally necessary the view that what a true elementary proposition describes must be an enduring individual, such as a human self; but there is the obvious alternative that what is described is an event, such as a human experience. Leibniz also assumes that the basic properties of a subject are non-relative ones, those not containing other subjects as constituents, as A's relation-to-B contains B; but there is obviously the alternative that every subject must have relative properties, and so possess other subjects as constituents. Again, Descartes assumes that mind is to be defined as inextended, leaving the necessity for a not-mind to explain extension; but, as Leibniz partly perceived and James, Peirce, and Whitehead have shown, it is conceivable that the web of relations between minds, or rather experiences, *is* extension. Again, the older rationalists assume that God must be conceived as at once supremely actual and supremely non-relative, "ab-

solute," or independent of becoming; whereas it is conceivable that the supreme actuality is precisely the supreme example of becoming and relativity.

On all these issues and many others, Whitehead is much more aware than his predecessors of the alternatives that may (with greater or less coherence and consistency) be held. If he asserts that events and experiences are the ultimate subjects of predication, it is not because it has never occurred to him to regard "things" and "persons" in this light; but because he believes he sees that two thousand years of persistent effort to achieve rational coherence by this method have failed and were bound to fail. These are just some of the ways in which Whitehead is more of a rationalist than his predecessors.

2. In spite, or because, of his genuine rationalism, Whitehead is also an empiricist who actually describes experience — and not some pseudo-rationalist myth about experience. Locke and Hume and Mill, for example, treat experience as though it were something assembled primarily (but not too successfully) for the mere purpose of cognitive mirroring of the world around the human body, rather than an enjoying, striving, sympathetic (yet partly antipathetic), responsive (yet partly self-creative) activity, whose primary intuitive data are its own past states, its intentions for the future, and the processes within its "body." Again, earlier empiricists treat memory and anticipation as secondary, as at most mere ways in which we know that existence is successive, instead of as constitutive features of our only intuited examples of that very successiveness itself. They speak also of experience as a duality of subject and object, of experiencing and what

is experienced, but never quite identify the two terms of this duality, since their "ideas" or "impressions" or "mental states" are equivocal in this regard. Or again, Hume contrasts self-interest and sympathy, but does not observe — what is certainly the case — that self-interest *is* a sort of sympathy whose objects are past and future experiences of the same human person. Nor did the "empiricists" (or Kant either) realize that, as Croce says, all direct intuition is expression of feeling or that the basic principles of immediate awareness are esthetic. Whitehead matches and surpasses the introspective subtlety of Bergson, Croce, and William James, and embodies the living process of experience in his philosophical description.

3. As a result of this descriptive accuracy, Whitehead is enabled to be perhaps the first realist who escapes from the ego-centric predicament and shows how he does it. R. B. Perry did not quite explain his own escape from the dilemma: either a thing is unknown to me or known to me; in the latter case, its being-known-to-me is apparently one of its properties, and hence, if I wish to know what the thing would be were it not known to me, I find myself trying to know without knowing.

Whitehead solves the problem by pointing out that real relatedness is given only as prehension — feeling of awareness of — and that the prehended does not prehend its prehender and hence is not really related to it. Thus in memory we prehend and are really related to past experience; but this does not relate the past experience to the present memory, for we certainly do not remember the past as having anticipated or prehended or in any way referred to this present memory of itself. Nor does present experience refer to any particular future memory of itself. Memory is thus the givenness of a relatedness that runs one way only, that has no actual converse. Accordingly, whereas Perry and C. I. Lewis say that the relation of being known by a certain subject is at any rate not important to a particular concrete object, Whitehead can say that it is (in a large class of cases, at least) simply *nothing* to the object. If this is realism, Whitehead is an absolute realist.

4. In spite, or even because, of this radical realism, Whitehead's theory is a thoroughgoing "idealism," if this means the doctrine that subjectivity is the principle of all being. Prehension being the actuality of relatedness, it is on the one hand established that to know a thing is to find, not to create, it — for we prehend actualities that do not prehend us — but on the other hand, since the actuality we know must have some relatedness to its world, it must prehend that world. Every singular actuality (for Whitehead, as for Leibniz, perceived extended things are collectives) must be related to — in other words must prehend — a world of antecedent actualities. In this regard, the actuality is a subject whose object is a world of antecedent subjects. But also, every actuality adds itself to the evergrowing totality of the real, which through it acquires a new member. In this regard, the actuality is a subject *about to become object* for subsequent subjects. The very status of being about-to-become-object is itself object for the actuality. An experience expects to become past for some new present, and this feeling of being about to become past (i.e., prehended by subjects not in the

world of the initial subject) is constitutive of all experience. Every actual occasion thus is, and feels itself
to be, a potential for objectification in future occasions.
But this potentiality, like all potentiality, need not be
actualized in just this way, or in just that way, by this
subject rather than by that, so long as it is actualized some-
how.

Or we may put Whitehead's discovery here as follows:
That an object is a potential for objectification blurs the
distinction between universal and particular.[1] For potentiality is universality. Any entity, O, involves the possibility, "some subject or other, any subject, prehending O";
but *any*-subject-prehending-O is a universal, of which *this*-
subject-prehending-O is a particular instance. Now, al-
though no universal can imply how it is to be particular-
ized in a given instance (for then it would be particular
and not universal), nevertheless, as Aristotle maintained,
the universal can have being only as it is concretized *some-
how*. Accordingly, that the object must be object for some
subject rather than none (though it need not be so for this
subject rather than that) illustrates the Aristotelian principle. (There can be fictitious or unembodied universals,
but they are complex and derivative from embodied universals. "Prehension of O" is not complex in the relevant
fashion — just as "about to become past" adds nothing to
"present.") I can indeed know what the thing known
would be though I myself did not know or feel it; but I cannot possibly know what it would be were it now unknown
and unfelt, any more than I can know what an existent
Platonic form would be were there nothing concrete to
embody it. All being is prehended as indifferent to the

---

1 See *Process and Reality,* p. 76.

particular prehension, but nothing is or could be prehended as indifferent to being prehended at all, for this would mean indifferent to being contained in any world at all, term of any real relatedness, past for any present. It is true also that there must be a divine present to endow an actuality with *adequate* objectivity, whereby with all its being it is immortally past — but this divine subjectivity (as here required) is not any *particular* subject.

This point will become clearer when the next three paragraphs have been read.

5. Whitehead is, in the Western world at least, the first great philosophical theist who, as a philosopher, really believes in the God of religion. (This statement may seem startling; it assumes that Socinus and Tertullian were not great philosophers; perhaps it is unjust to Fechner and the later Schelling.) The God of religion is a supreme person capable of relations to other persons, or at any rate — for the word "person" is not the point — one who knows, loves, and wills with regard to others who know, love, and will. A person is given not as a particular actuality, but as a *principle of sequence* of actualities. The principle is the personality or character of the individual, the actualities are the states, experiences, or acts expressing that character.

No great philosopher before Whitehead put this manifest fact of experience in clear technical terms. Personality is the "defining characteristic" of a "society of occasions" in linear temporal ("personal") order, these occasions being the successive experiences actualizing the individual in question. The defining characteristic is less concrete or particular than its expressions; it has a certain abstractness or neutrality with respect to alternative possible experiences and acts. Philip drunk or Philip sober is still Philip, but obviously not the same determinate or particular actuality. The extreme contrast to the universal or general is not the individual but the particular. The individual is intermediate, semi-abstract, partially unparticular or indeterminate. If it were otherwise, a man's character at birth plus his environment would entail all his future actions, and he would be in the iron grip of determinations effected before he could do anything much about them. Also, we would not know who John Jones was unless we could predict all his future experiences. The very function of proper names would be nullified. The traditional view of God as identical in his actuality with his character or "essence" entirely deprives him of freedom, personality, or individuality, and makes him either a meaningless universal embodied in nothing concrete, or a meaningless particular expressing no character, purpose, or individuality.

Whitehead, by distinguishing between the primordial essence or personality, and the consequent state or actuality (he probably should not have called it "nature") of deity is almost the first to deal seriously with the individuality of God. The primordial essence is absolute, independent, abstract, and (like everything abstract) neutral with respect to particular determinations. The essence is "infinite" and non-actual. *All* personal character, indeed, is abstract, neutral, free from wholly determinate limits, and is a principle or potency of actualization, rather than any actual entity; but divine personality is unique and transcendent in quality by being absolutely (instead of only relatively) abstract, infinitely (instead of only finitely) free or indeterminate, with respect to particularization.

But, whereas earlier metaphysicians generally stopped here, leaving deity a mere unlimited essence, totally devoid of definite actuality, a power totally divorced from expression or achievement, Whitehead adds the other side of the divine portrait. The consequent actuality of deity is the sequence of determinate, contingent experiences expressing both the essence of deity and the *de facto* content of the world God experiences at a given moment. Whereas the divine essence is "absolute," impassive, the consequent actuality is "relative" and passive, with a supreme sensitivity or responsiveness that is, without equivocation, love itself in unadulterated purity.

This is the first clear-headedly honest intellectualization (for Schelling's and Fechner's analyses are less clear) of what religion has always intuitively meant by "God."

6. Whitehead, more than any other, has really "answered Hume." By his account of memory and physical purpose, generalized in his "reformed subjectivism," by his explanation of order in terms of esthetic drives, focused in God, Whitehead gives causality a uniquely adequate grounding. He furnishes the "impressions" of causal connectedness that Hume calls for, and at the same time, by showing the subtlety of these impressions and the complexity of the problem of causality and induction, which is only solved (as Hume indeed suspected — see his *Dialogues*) when all main factors, including God, are reckoned with, Whitehead justifies Hume's refusal to be satisfied with solutions then available.

7. Whitehead is the first to embody modern relational logic in a fairly complete metaphysical system. (Peirce

perhaps came nearest to anticipating this achievement.)
Logic has discovered itself to be the study of relational
structures as involved in meanings. Metaphysics ought to
be the study of relational structure as embodied in reality
as such, or taken generically. Instead of focusing on the
meager, arbitrarily limited question of how particular
actualities are related to universal properties, how an *S*
is *P*, we need to focus on the general case of how actualities,
as such, are related to actualities of the past, and to poten-
tialities for future actualization; or how a subject is self-
referent to other subjects, in both their particular and their
universal aspects. This is what the theory of prehensions
effects. By the ontological principle (perhaps sometimes
forgotten in Whitehead's exposition), relationship to other
actualities includes all relationships and is the general case.
This is what the Aristotelian doctrine of the universal-
only-in-the-particular comes to, when we face the necessity
that things must have relative properties.

The Philosophy of Organism here retains the old truth
that properties must actually qualify something actual,
some subject, but adds the new truth that we must recognize relational properties — those by which some portion
of the system of particular things enters into the nature
of each thing, and thus there is "immanence" of one thing
in another. Yet Whitehead avoids the modern error of
Absolute Idealism which would impose no limitations
upon this immanence, and make all things constituents
of each thing. At this point, Whitehead follows the sound
lead of G. E. Moore and William James in defending the
thesis of "external" relatedness,[2] but without forgetting —

---

[2] Whitehead, *Science and the Modern World* (1925), pp. 174-75, 223;
Adventures of Ideas (1933), pp. 247-256; *Process and Reality* (1929), p.

as Moore at least did forget — that every real relation must be "somewhere," in some actuality, internal to some term, though by no necessity to all terms. Thus, undeterred either by the specious simplicity of the ancient subject-predicate logic, or by the current logical fiction that "every relation has a converse," Whitehead seeks and finds the ways in which a thing may be self-referent to another thing, without the second thing having any reference to the first, so that *a R b* is an actual relatedness, while *b R a* is not. In this way, he arrives at the objective analogue of the relational structure of meanings, in a theory of partly self-creative, partly caused or derivative atomic creatures, self-referent to the world they are about to enrich.

This is the first theory of time worthy of the name. For it is the first that ascribes to time an intelligible logical structure, while allowing for a principle of flux or passage that transcends all fixed or already determinate structures, since it is an inexhaustible source of new relationships, extrinsic to reality as already actual.

8. Whitehead is among the first to see the philosophical generality inherent in the principle of evolution, the principle that the characters of things, as expressed in their

---

470. It is true that Whitehead mainly emphasizes internal rather than external relations, partly because he is primarily combatting not Absolute Idealism (which has been somewhat out of fashion) but rather atomistic and other more or less extreme pluralisms. Also, I suspect, he inclines (as a rule, not always) to avoid the phrase "external relations" because, to say "relation to *B* is external to *A*" is really to say, "*A* has no relation to *B*." (See chap. 2 of my *The Divine Relativity*, Yale University Press, 1948.) An entity's relations are all internal to the entity, but it does not follow that *X*'s relations to *Y* must all be internal *to Y*. A relation may involve terms not all of which involve the relation. And Whitehead in effect holds that no actuality ever has relation to a particular actuality subsequent to it in time.

ways of acting, are products of change; and to see that this enables us to dispense with the mythical notion of laws as eternally fixed, yet quantitatively definite, aspects of behavior. It is enough for us if nature changes sufficiently slowly in her more basic ways — those whose duration defines a "cosmic epoch" — for all our needs of prediction and mental reconstruction of the past. Whitehead also avoids the arbitrariness of Peirce's view that the world gets more and more orderly. One order may change to another, but "more" or "less" orderly is an unwarranted, if not absurd, addition.

9. Most philosophers seem to regard the discovery of cells in biology as merely a tale told to them when they were young. For they speak of the body as though it were essentially one entity, one mass of stuff, or machine, or "material" aspect of one human individual. In fact, the body is a vast "society of cells," none of which is a human being, and any of which could (with minor modifications) conceivably exist and live in a suitable medium outside of any human organism.

Whitehead seems to be among the first to see that all this renders imperative a generalization of the idea of "environment," if that means, "the set of individuals with which a given individual interacts." The body is nothing but the most necessary, inseparable, intimate portion of our social environment, or field-of-relationships with *other* living beings, each living its own life. Whitehead draws the consequence that the primary non-human (and non-divine) datum of human experience must be cellular activity, objectified without distinctness as to individual cells, and instinctively taken as an index of conditions outside the bodily system, an index whose general reliability is due to evolutionary adaptation.

This view appears to fit every known fact. And at one stroke it explains both how we know sub-human reality, and how we are causally influenced by such reality. For the subject could not be uninfluenced by what it directly, even though indistinctively, intuits. This is a part of Whitehead's "answer to Hume."

10. Who before Whitehead presented a clear, fully-articulated reason for temporal atomicity, a special quantitative illustration of which is given by quantum mechanics? Or for the wave structure pervasive in nature, which for Whitehead illustrates (though it would not, unless in extremely generalized form, be deducible from) the esthetic laws of contrast and repetition to which all appetition is subject?[3]

11. Whitehead seems to be the only philosopher to note the universality of societies in the cosmos, at all levels; also, and best of all, he is the first to see that what is called an individual in common life (and much philosophy) can only be understood as a *form of sequence* of particular actualities socially inheriting common quality from antecedent members; and that personality itself is a special temporally linear case of such social — that is, sympathetic — inheritance. Thus the account of personal self-identity which modern psychology substitutes for the pseudo-simplicity of the "soul" is integrated into a comprehensive generalization that is superlative in its sweep — apparently too much so for pedestrian minds. The ethical problem

---

[3] See *Process and Reality*, p. 426.

of self-interest and altruism can, really for the first time, now be analyzed without radical ambiguity as to *what* "self" is in question. Self-interest, so far as looking to the future, is seen as a case of sympathetic projection, not radically different from some other cases of such projection.

12. Whitehead is among the first to see that empiricism means the necessity of generalizing comparative psychology and sociology downwards to include physiology, biology, chemistry, and physics as studies of the more elementary types of sentient individuals and societies. Biology has already begun to follow this lead. Agar shows how embryology, for example, is best conceived as the study of the responsive behavior of cells under the stimulus of a highly specialized environment (in the womb) .[4]

Some readers will of course feel that the foregoing estimate of Whitehead depends for most of its plausibility upon the assumption that the universe really is the sort of social process of "feelings of feelings" that Whitehead thinks it is. I venture three remarks here.

Whitehead certainly has not chosen this view because of inattention to its alternatives. He obviously knows why the idea of mere matter, or "vacuous actuality," for example, has appealed to so many. Quite a portion of his life must have been passed in meditation upon this question, meditation focused upon the main facts of modern science and the main trends of modern philosophy.

Also, the sole way to refute Whitehead's declaration —

---

[4] W. E. Agar, *A Contribution to the Theory of the Living Organism* (Melbourne, 1943) .

that we shall never succeed in elaborating an explanatory metaphysics until we have stopped trying to include in such a system the alleged concept of vacuous actuality — the sole way to refute this negative prediction is to produce a metaphysics which accepts vacuous actuality and which yet rivals Whitehead's in coherence and width of applicability to experience.

Third, to the complaint (which Morris Cohen and others have expressed) that modern science, far from having eliminated the concept of matter, has rather arrived at a more subtle and adequate one, and thus has confirmed "materialism" instead of refuting it, the answer is that so far as matter means vacuous actuality, no such concept functions in science at all. In other terms, if "matter" means something *alternative to experience* (to subjectivity in the broadest sense) , then precisely this alternative status, this *definitely asserted possibility* of no-experience, no feeling, no-sociality, this alleged neutrality or possible vacuousness of matter, by which it was formerly contrasted to mind, is the very set of aspects, or pseudo-notions, that advances in scientific subtlety and adequacy have been eliminating, until, as Whitehead says, not one such aspect remains. Physics does, to be sure, need the notion of physical reality, reality with spatio-temporal characters, and this notion Whitehead accepts along with science and common sense. But since, according to his observations and analysis, experiences as such have spatio-temporal characters, and since no unmistakable samples of concrete actuality other than experiences are directly given or positively imaginable as actualities (with quality as well as relational structure, causal connectedness, intrinsic becoming, etc.) , it is, he holds, meaningless to say that besides experiences there are also the merely physical realities. Experiences *are* physical realities, and our only way of positively generalizing the notion of "real" or "physical actuality," beyond the specific traits of human experiences as sample realities, is to generalize the notion of experience itself so as to enable it to include a vast and indeed infinite range of possible types of non-human experience, not forgetting divine experience. If this cannot be done, then we are incurably ignorant of what can be meant by "real" or "process" in general, as we must certainly be of any positive characters distinguishing the parts of nature to which we deny the characters of experience.

A difficult concept in Whitehead is that of the Creativity, or the ultimate ground, or substantial activity. Is this a sort of God beyond God? I have some doubt whether all his utterances on this topic can be reconciled. But we are told that the creativity is not an actual or concrete entity. My suggestion is that we regard creativity or the principle of process as an "analogical concept" functioning in Whitehead's system somewhat as "being" functions in Aristotelian theology. There are diverse kinds of being, according to Thomas Aquinas, with a major division between the necessary being of God and the contingent being of all else. So, for Whitehead, it is impossible simply to identify creative action with divine action because *every* actual entity, as partly "self-created," has its own action. (This, of course, is one aspect of the explanation of how evil results from action.) Moreover, the divine action is unique because, just as the divine being in Thomism was held to exist necessarily and eternally, so in Whitehead-ianism the divine process, since it is, in its primordial aspect, the ground of all possibility (the eternal objects), is likewise necessary, in the sense that it is not a possibility that there should be no such process, and this distinguishes it from ordinary kinds of process. Thus creativity-as-such is no more a God beyond God in this system than being-as-such is in Thomism. The difference is mainly in the shift from mere being to process — as the ultimate analogical universal or form of forms.

My own conviction is that if there is anything in the passages dealing with this topic not capable of the foregoing interpretation, it probably ought to be discarded, and would have been discarded by Whitehead himself, had his attention been brought to bear a little more fully upon the question. My only alternative or supplementary suggestion is that one or two of the remarks about creativity might possibly be applied to God instead, on condition that they do not contradict the basic primordial-consequent structure attributed to deity.

In conclusion, one may say that the basic principles of our knowledge and experience, physical, biological, sociological, esthetic, religious, are in this philosophy given an intellectual integration such as only a thousand or ten thousand years of further reflection and inquiry seem likely to exhaust or adequately evaluate, but whose wide relevance and in many respects at least comparative accuracy some of us think can already be discerned.

Whitehead's Philosophy of Civilization

By A. H. JOHNSON

WHITEHEAD'S PRE-EMINENCE in logic, the philosophy of science, and metaphysics has tended to distract attention from his genuine achievements in other fields. This is particularly true with reference to his study of civilization. It is both strange and unfortunate that the general and the philosophic public are relatively unaware of his work in this area. In truth, Whitehead's philosophy of civilization is a major scene in the broad tapestry of his philosophic system. Further, his contributions merit careful consideration.

In a very real sense, Whitehead's three most important books are concerned with this topic. The fact is clearly emphasized in the preface of each of these books. For instance, in *Science and the Modern World* he states: "The present book involves a study of some aspects of Western culture during the past three centuries, in so far as it has been influenced by the development of science."[1] *Adventures of Ideas* provides a more general survey. "The book is in fact a study of the concept of civilization, and an endeavor to understand how it is that civilized beings arise."[2] Even the technically awesome *Process and Reality*

---

[1] *Science and the Modern World* (New York: Macmillan Co., 1929) , p. ix.
[2] *Adventures of Ideas* (New York: Macmillan Co., 1933) , p. vii.

is designed to formulate a set of concepts "adequate for the interpretation of the ideas and problems which form the complex texture of civilized thought."[3] He returns to the topic of civilization in his last book, *Modes of Thought.* It is obviously involved in his *Aims of Education* and in many of the articles that he wrote for the *Atlantic Monthly* and other journals. Further, those who had personal contact with Professor Whitehead quickly became aware of his great interest in the problems of civilized living, not only in the area of theory, but also in the realm of practice. Indeed one would have to search long and vigorously to find a more civilized person than Alfred North Whitehead. Granted then that he was interested in civilization and proposed to undertake a study of this topic, the question arises: What specific contributions did he make?

In the first place, he provides a simple definition of civilization. Secondly, he suggests how civilization may be established or strengthened. Thirdly, he notes that his theory of reality is such that the possibility of civilization is not denied by the nature of things.

Whitehead states that a civilized society is characterized by a deep concern for truth, beauty, adventure, art, and peace.[4] The key terms of this definition require some clarification. His extremely technical discussion of the concepts of truth and beauty need not be examined in this paper. Suffice it to say that in general he advocates the correspondence theory of "truth," and contends that "beauty" is characterized by patterned contrast. He defines "adventure" as the search for new perfection. It is

[3] *Process and Reality* (New York: Macmillan Co., 1929), p. v.
[4] *Adventures of Ideas,* p. 353.

not just a matter of geographical exploration. Creative initiative must be manifest in all spheres of human activity — or civilization vanishes. The blind worship of the good old days, and ways, is the funeral service of civilization.

The term "peace" has a rather technical meaning. It is not the mere absence of strife, internal, industrial or international. It is a genuine immunity to the distractions of fame and fortune, and, in general, the many things which ordinarily make our lives miserable. It is achieved by those who forget their own merely selfish interests in the pursuit of exalted goals. Peace arises from the conviction that what is worth while is not in vain.

The mention of "art" as a defining quality of civilization may seem strange. What Whitehead means is this: Art expresses truth and beauty. Art also serves as a stimulating reminder of the powers of human creativity. Contemplation of art is one of the means of achieving peace. Thus it is Whitehead's opinion that unless these various artistic functions are performed, civilization does not exist. To repeat — he contends that a civilized society is one characterized by the qualities truth, beauty, adventure, art, and peace. It is to be noted that the quality "goodness" is also involved even though Whitehead does not specifically list it.

In order to achieve this type of society, certain conditions must be present. Fundamental among these is the necessity of properly appreciating the value of each individual human being. This issues in the toleration — indeed the encouragement — of a wide range of individual differences. Whitehead admits that exceptional behavior may be ridiculous or even dangerous; he feels, however, that the risks are justified by the benefits which sometimes accrue. This respect for different thoughts and actions should be manifest not only within a nation but also in the sphere of international relations. As he aptly expresses the matter: "A diversification among human communities is essential for the providing of the incentive and the material for the Odyssey of the human spirit."[5] This leads to the claim that civilization ultimately cannot be based on the use of force. Civilization is characterized by devotion to high ideals. It involves the tolerant appreciation of extreme individual differences. Civilization, therefore, must rely on rational persuasion rather than force. Reliance on force tends to produce anesthesia with reference to the higher values of life. There is frequently a narrow concentration of interest on the obvious pleasures of the senses. Whitehead with characteristic irony remarks: "It is the nemesis of the reign of force, of the worship of power" that attention centers "upon some variant of Solomon's magnificent harem of three hundred wives and seven hundred concubines. The variation may be toward decency, but it is equally decadent."[6]

The preceding references to respect for individual differences and the reliance on persuasion should not mislead one into thinking that Whitehead has no place for compulsion in his analysis of civilized living. Human rights are subject to limitations. There are correlative duties. Ultimately the welfare of society must be the decisive factor. By way of clarification, he expresses general approval (apart from his condemnation of the institution of slavery) of the mingling of individual liberty and environ-

---

[5] *Science and the Modern World,* p. 298.

[6] *Adventures of Ideas,* p. 108.

mental compulsion in the idealized Athens of Pericles as described by Thucydides.

Underlying these conditions, and productive of them, there must be a specific type of education. Obviously, it will center on the co-operative satisfaction of individual needs and interests. There must be a fruitful balance of theory and practice, fact and ideal. It must be the type of education which issues in "insight and foresight and a sense of the worth of life."[7]

Having defined civilization and stated some of the major conditions for its achievement, Whitehead realistically examines decisive social factors in order to determine whether these conditions can be really established. In his opinion, the decisive social factors are: (a) ideas, (b) great men, (c) economic activities, (d) the inanimate world. He declines to assign ultimate efficacy to any one of these factors. They are inescapably interrelated. That is to say, civilization exists only when men accept the ideals (ideas) of civilization and regulate their economic activities and the process of inanimate nature in accordance with these ideals.

Some of the practical implications of this position are indicated. For example, Whitehead is greatly impressed by the efficacy of ideas. *Science and the Modern World* traces the tremendous impact of scientific ideas on all phases of life. *Adventures of Ideas* provides an impressive indication of the effect of the idea of "the intellectual and moral grandeur of the human soul." He contends that as we think, so we live. In other words, civilization is impossible unless the ideals of civilization are clearly

---

7 *Adventures of Ideas*, p. 125.

before us. It is to be noted that Whitehead is not guilty of fuzzy optimism at this point. He recognizes that ideals work very slowly. There is no immediate magic which dwells within clearly formulated ideals. The ideas must be understood, accepted, and applied by human beings.

Obviously then, men are important factors in the achievement of civilization. Not only do they formulate and spread its ideals, but men who manifest these ideals serve as a stimulus to others. Whitehead mentions men who have functioned in this fashion: Socrates, Jesus, Newton, and — in our day — John Dewey. While he stresses the impact of men with ideas, Whitehead does not disregard the importance of men of military inclinations. In some instances military leaders provide conditions of peace which make possible the achievement of civilization.

Proceeding to a discussion of other important social factors, Whitehead emphasizes the fact that, of course, men and ideas do not function in a vacuum. There are inanimate factors. Men must have food and shelter. There are the forces of nature. He fully recognizes the importance of geographical location and climate. It is suggested that "civilization haunts the borders of waterways."[8] Personality traits of Englishmen differ depending on the part of the country in which they live. Indeed, he goes so far as to say: "Geography is half of character."[9] Yet, having developed this point, Whitehead with customary balance concludes that such factors are only part of the total causal nexus.

Turning next to a consideration of economic activities,

---

8 "Harvard: The Future," *The Atlantic Monthly*, CLVIII, 260.
9 "The Education of an Englishman," *The Atlantic Monthly*, CXXXVIII, 193.

it is to be observed that Whitehead is well aware of the importance of technological developments. For example, the use of steam as a means of power made it much easier to abolish the institution of slavery. The spread of ideas made possible by the invention of the printing press is another important fact facilitating the rise of civilization. In general, Whitehead emphasizes the point that true civilization can only be achieved if industry is directed in such a fashion that *all* concerned may experience the distinctive qualities of civilized living; truth, beauty, art, adventure, and peace.

So far this essay has been concerned with (a) Whitehead's definition of civilization, and (b) his analysis of the conditions and factors which must be considered in connection with the practical problem of establishing or improving civilization. There remain a number of critical questions to be considered. For instance, this: Does he regard the present economic system as being conducive to a high degree of civilization? The answer is an emphatic "no." His analysis of the implications of our system clearly indicates its woeful inadequacy as a basis for civilized living, for most of those concerned. It is noted that under ordinary economic conditions, a considerable proportion of the population is not satisfactorily employed. That is to say, income is inadequate and/or the type of work being done does not satisfy basic needs and interests. In many cases there is merely a deadening routine of trifling operations. There is little or no place for the characteristic qualities of civilization. This is so not only for workers in industry; it also applies, to a considerable extent, to those who purchase the products of industry. A few "standard lines" are available in all the goods necessary for life. Little or no real initiative is involved in merchandizing. Beauty is lost or degraded. Truth and peace of mind wilt under the glare of modern advertising.

If this be the case, one may legitimately inquire: What remedial suggestions does Whitehead offer? It must be admitted that his discussion, at this point, suffers from considerable generality and is perhaps overly optimistic. Be that as it may, he states that, to begin with, the "business mind" must widen its range of interests. It must realize that business is only a part of the complex structure of human living. We will never have a civilized society as long as businessmen and others concentrate only on making money. He notes that unregulated, completely selfish competition produces something very like industrial slavery in modern society. He does not necessarily advocate the abandonment of huge corporations, private property, or mass production. His point is that these institutions must be operated in a different fashion. Men must have more opportunities to do creative work, diversified and satisfying. This, Whitehead admits, may involve a partial return to craftsmanship; he argues that experiences in French industry indicate that this is practical in some instances.[10] It is interesting to note that this apparently soft, sentimental approach is along the line of recommendations made by some modern efficiency experts. That is to say, unless a man enjoys his work and feels that it is worth doing, he will not do it well. Thus it seems possible to achieve both efficiency and a closer approach to the conditions of civilized living.

The point may be raised that Whitehead does not

---

[10] See *Adventures of Ideas,* chap. 6; *Science and the Modern World,* chap. 13; "The Study of the Past," *Harvard Business Review,* XI, 436-44.

deal adequately with the problem of keeping individual
diversities within reasonable limits. His references to
the Athens of Pericles may seem not particularly effective.
However, it should be noted that he also discusses the
problem in a modern setting. He suggests that control
over an individual, in certain areas of his behavior, should
be exercised by the professional group to which he be-
longs. This regulation would be effective in the area
of professional competence. Once a person's competence
in a field is established, then he is free to develop theories
and practices which are perhaps different from those of
the majority. It is not opinions and techniques which
are controlled. It is a case of determining whether the
person concerned has a solid enough foundation to make
adequate use of his freedom.

In the sphere of general behavior, the state, in so far
as it embodies the general wisdom of the community,
should exert a controlling influence. However, the basis
of its efficacy should not be brute strength. Rather the
true justification for governmental control is effectiveness,
as recognized by rational men. To repeat, it is Whitehead's opinion that the state has no business interfering in
matters of specifically professional or technical concern.
Medical doctors should certify the competence of medical
doctors. Teachers should determine the reliability of
teachers. To be specific, he suggests that the State of
Tennessee "exhibited a gross ignorance of its proper functions when it defied a professional opinion [concerning
evolution] which throughout the world is practically
unanimous."[11] It is, of course, obvious that many men
do not belong to professional groups in the narrow sense

---

[11] *Adventures of Ideas*, p. 78.

of the term. However, if the term be enlarged to include labor unions, the applicability of this suggestion is greatly increased.

Whitehead's discussion of the place of Palestine in the modern world was a sample of his attempt to grapple with a complex international problem in a civilized fashion. He began by stating that "the question at issue is not the happiness of a finite group. It is the fate of our civilization."[12] He reminded us that the Jews were not the only group who had been unpopular because of their creative initiative. In the eighteenth century the Scotch were in a similar situation, with reference to the English. Turning to practical recommendations, Whitehead suggested that the Jews be given "homelands" both in Palestine and elsewhere. He pointed to the long history of Jewish and Moslem co-operation in the Middle East to support his contention that it was possible again, in Palestine.

The civilized approach to a problem involves a reference to high ideals. This Whiteheadian conviction is clearly manifest in a brief letter written to the editor of *The Boston Globe,* on December 24, 1940:

> Many eminent people, including highly respected Harvard professors, have published reasons why American activity should be restricted to defense within her borders. We know how the Priest and the Levite explained to their friends their conduct during their famous walk from Jerusalem to Jericho. They were influenced by three reasons: (1) The assault happened on "the other side"; (2) They had an inherited distrust of Samaria; (3) After the incident had blown over, a profit-

---

12 "An Appeal to Sanity," *The Atlantic Monthly,* CLXIII, 315.

able trade could be carried on with the thieves. These considerations justify the Priest and the Levite if we put aside the moral issues upon which the parable insists. In the present case the moral issue is the defense of freedom.

When his "Appeal to Sanity" essay was reprinted shortly before his death, Whitehead added a footnote which emphasizes the same general point. He stated that after seven years of wartime experience he was convinced that the future of civilization depends on a moral approach to all problems. There must be a spirit of sympathetic compromise, the sort of attitude which is embodied in the *ideals* of the United Nations organization.[13]

Here, then, are a few samples of the suggestions offered by Whitehead as to how a civilized person should approach modern problems. These suggestions fall into the areas of economic activity, freedom and compulsion in social groups, the Palestine problem, and the problem of international relations. His comments are not always as specific as one would wish, but even these relatively general statements clarify his point of view and provoke thought.

It will be obvious from the foregoing that Whitehead's philosophy of civilization is not pessimistic. For him the term "civilization" is not synonymous with decadence and disaster. He argues that a true civilization is characterized by adventure, the continuous pursuit of new excellences. A civilized society will change to meet new challenges. Its traditional methods of thought and action will not be worshiped blindly; they will be revised as the need arises.

---

13 See *Essays in Science and Philosophy,* p. 53.

The flower of a true civilization never fades. More specifically he reminds us that the list of forces "inevitably destined to destroy our civilization" has a very familiar sound; in the past men have misused material power, have been blind to higher values, etc. Yet at least a measure of civilization has survived. Whitehead could see no reason why the struggle for survival might not continue to be successful. This is not to deny the seriousness of the present situation. Whitehead's point is that the destruction of civilization is not inevitable.[14]

Finally, it is important to note that Whitehead's philosophy of civilization is consistent with his general metaphysical position. His analysis of civilization stresses value, the importance of the individual, creative change (adventure), mutual tolerance, persuasion rather than force, peace. It will be recalled that his theory of actual entities involves all these emphases. An actual entity is an individual, essentially concerned with value experience. It is continually engaged in a creative process of interaction with others. This involves persuasion, not force. Actual entities are fundamentally related to entities beyond themselves. What is of supreme value is preserved ultimately in God. Thus, the state of peace is possible. This is not to say that Whitehead contends that each actual entity is civilized. His point is this: The possibility of achieving civilization (given suitable conditions) is not ruled out by the nature of reality.

In the years of his maturity Whitehead undertook to frame a coherent, logical, necessary system of general ideas such that everything would be a particular instance of that scheme. In the preceding paragraph I have sug-

---

14 See *Adventures of Ideas*, pp. 359-60.

gested that this project was carried out in his philosophy of civilization. Be that as it may, the main purpose of this essay has been to show that his achievements were not confined to logic, philosophy of science, and metaphysics. He was profoundly interested in the complex problems of social relationship. He performed a very useful service in providing a brief, clear definition of civilization, a reminder of the fundamental importance of truth, beauty, goodness, adventure, art, and peace. Of at least equal importance is his analysis of the conditions and factors which make civilized living possible. He offers suggestions concerning the civilized approach to some of our pressing modern problems. All this is an integral and essential part of the great twentieth-century intellectual synthesis — the philosophy of Alfred North Whitehead.

Index